Del McCool

CW01510732

The Modern Civil War Survival Guide

Author: Del McCool

Editor: San-del Team

San-del Writers LLC

Revision 2.0

eBook ISBN:

Paperback ISBN: 979-8-9900113-3-5

Hardcover ISBN:

Cover artist:

Matt -SurviveOffline.com

Disclaimer

Please note the information contained within this book is for educational and entertainment purposes only. All efforts have been made to present accurate, up-to-date, reliable, and complete information. No warranties of any kind are declared or implied. Readers acknowledge that the author is not engaging in the rendering of legal, financial, medical, or professional advice. The contents of this book have been derived from various sources. Please consult a licensed professional before attempting any techniques outlined in this book.

Dedications

Thanks to my loyal readers for supporting me in publishing this book.

Special thanks to my wife Sandra and family.

Contents

Preface

This book, *The Modern Civil War Survival Guide*, is intended for educational purposes only.

1. **Historical Context:** No country has ever welcomed the prospect of armed conflict among its citizens, and the United States is no exception. Throughout history, civil wars have been a last resort when it seemed that armed conflict was the only way to resolve issues or perceived issues within a sovereign country.

2. **Survival Considerations:** Survival is something every person needs to consider. Think about a natural disaster like a hurricane, tornado, or flood. People are often without power and water for days. Gas stations and stores become useless, resulting in long lines and panicked people. It may take weeks to return to normalcy. Now, imagine this scenario caused by a

domestic terrorist bombing and potential shootings. People would hide in their homes with no power or food, afraid to go outside. This is more likely to be the starting point of a modern civil war, rather than large-scale armies clashing.

3. **Key Factors Leading to Armed Conflict:** These five key factors often lead people to consider armed reactions when rational means of resolution fail:

1. Entrenched national polarization with no clear path to resolution.
2. Increasingly divisive press coverage and information flows, resulting in extreme media polarization.
3. Weakened institutions, notably Congress and the judiciary.
4. Political leadership abandoning their responsibilities to voters.
5. The legitimization of violence as an acceptable method for conducting discourse or solving disputes.

4. **Global Civil War Precedents:** In recent years, these factors have triggered civil wars in other countries, such as:

   1. Fighting between ethnic groups.

   2. Fighting between religious groups.

   3. Fighting over historic land ownership.

   4. Large groups feel they are losing status in their country.

   5. Examples include conflicts in Yugoslavia, Serbia, Bosnia, Ethiopia, and Northern Ireland.

      - In 1948, the Colombian Civil War occurred between liberals and conservatives and lasted ten years.

5. **Potential Flashpoints in the U.S.:** Issues in the U.S. that could ignite civil conflict include:

   1. Local political issues that should be handled locally or at the state level are

being overridden by the federal level with no recourse.

2. Citizens' identities are becoming increasingly tied to their political beliefs.

3. Social media amplifies issues on both the right and left.

4. Growing militancy and radicalism on both sides of political issues, with social media inflaming the situation instead of defusing it.

5. Political polarization leading to the formation and training of militia-like insurgency groups on both sides.

6. Small groups of domestic terrorists from either side carry out bombings or kidnappings, causing fear and panic nationwide, further polarizing and radicalizing the population.

7. Constant exposure to violence leads citizens to live in fear both inside and outside their homes.

8. The prevalence of guns in many households and the ability to acquire more as needed.

9. Small-scale attacks on any group could trigger widespread violent responses, potentially overwhelming local law enforcement and state national guards, taxing federal resources, and creating lawless enclaves. This could lead to the collapse of state and federal governments.

10. A lack of trust in national election results by either group.

Please use this book as a tool to educate yourself on the many things to be aware of in a civil war situation.

Author: Del McCool

- **U.S. Army Veteran – 10 years**
- **Law Enforcement Veteran – 14 years**

Chapter 1

Understanding Modern Civil Wars

The Evolution of Civil Wars in the Modern Era

In the modern era, civil wars have evolved significantly from their historical counterparts. Today, civil wars are characterized by several unique factors that make them particularly challenging to navigate and survive. From technological advancements in warfare to the use of cyber warfare and drones, the landscape of civil conflicts has changed dramatically in recent years.

One of the key aspects of modern civil wars is the use of urban warfare tactics and strategies. In densely populated areas, traditional military tactics are often ineffective, leading to the development of new strategies that focus on controlling key infrastructure and population centers.

This shift has had a profound impact on the way civil wars are fought and the potential risks that civilians face in these environments.

Technological advancements in warfare have also played a significant role in shaping modern civil conflicts. From the use of drones and unmanned aerial vehicles to the development of sophisticated cyber warfare capabilities, combatants in civil wars now have access to tools that were once the stuff of science fiction.

These advancements have not only changed the way wars are fought but have also raised new ethical and legal questions about the use of these technologies in conflict.

Cyber warfare is another critical aspect of modern civil wars that cannot be overlooked. As conflicts increasingly play out in cyberspace, the implications for civilians and combatants alike are profound.

From the spread of misinformation and propaganda to the disruption of critical infrastructure, cyber warfare has the potential to shape the outcome of conflicts in ways that were previously unimaginable.

In addition to these technological advancements, the role of private military companies, the impact of social media, and the environmental consequences of modern civil wars are all factors that must be considered when preparing for and navigating these conflicts.

By understanding the evolving nature of civil wars in the modern era, individuals can better prepare themselves for the challenges that lie ahead and increase their chances of survival in an increasingly complex and dangerous world.

Common Triggers for Civil Conflicts

Civil conflicts can be triggered by a variety of factors, many of which are common across different regions and contexts. Understanding these triggers is essential for anyone looking to prepare for the possibility of civil war in their area.

One common trigger for civil conflicts is political instability, which can arise from corrupt or ineffective government leadership, disputed elections, or long-standing grievances among different ethnic or religious groups.

These issues can create a sense of injustice and inequality that fuels resentment and can lead to violent clashes.

Another common trigger for civil conflicts is economic hardship, such as high unemployment rates, inflation, or food shortages.

When people are struggling to make ends meet and provide for their families, they may be more likely to join armed groups or engage in violent protests as a way to demand change.

Social inequality, including disparities in wealth, access to resources, and opportunities for education and employment, can also contribute to feelings of resentment and fuel tensions between different social groups.

Ethnic or religious divisions are another common trigger for civil conflicts, as these differences can be exploited by political leaders or armed groups seeking to mobilize support for their cause. The perception of discrimination or marginalization based on one's ethnicity or religion can create a sense of identity-based conflict that is difficult to resolve through peaceful means.

In some cases, historical grievances or unresolved disputes over land or resources can also serve as triggers for violence and instability.

In addition to these traditional triggers for civil conflicts, modern warfare tactics and technologies have also played a role in escalating violence in many contemporary conflicts.

The use of drones and unmanned aerial vehicles, for example, has made it easier for armed groups to carry out targeted attacks on enemy forces or civilian populations, often with devastating consequences.

Cyber warfare, including the use of hacking and propaganda campaigns to manipulate public opinion or disrupt critical infrastructure, has also become a significant factor in modern conflicts.

As civilians, it is important to be aware of these common triggers for civil conflicts and to take steps to prepare ourselves and our communities for the possibility of violence. This may include developing emergency plans, stocking up on essential supplies, and staying informed about potential threats in our area. By understanding the factors that can lead to civil war and taking proactive measures to protect ourselves and our loved ones, we can increase our chances of surviving and thriving in an increasingly unstable world.

Trends in Modern Civil Warfare

In recent years, there have been significant trends in modern civil warfare that have changed the landscape of conflict around the world. From urban warfare tactics to technological advancements in warfare, these trends have had a profound impact on how civil wars are fought and the strategies needed to survive them.

This subchapter will explore some of the key trends in modern civil warfare that adults should be aware of in order to better prepare for potential conflicts.

One of the most significant trends in modern civil warfare is the shift towards urban warfare tactics and strategies. As more conflicts take place in densely populated urban areas, combatants are forced to adapt their tactics to navigate the complexities of fighting in cities. This trend has led to increased civilian casualties and destruction of infrastructure, making it essential for adults to understand the unique challenges of urban warfare in order to protect themselves and their families.

Another trend in modern civil warfare is the rapid advancement of technology in warfare. From drones and unmanned aerial vehicles to sophisticated weaponry and surveillance systems, technology has fundamentally changed the way conflicts are fought. Adults must stay informed about the latest technological advancements in warfare in order to effectively prepare for and respond to modern civil wars.

Cyber warfare is another trend that has emerged in modern civil conflicts, with combatants using digital tactics to disrupt infrastructure, spread propaganda, and gather intelligence. The implications of cyber warfare in civil conflicts are vast, and adults must be aware of the potential threats posed by cyber-attacks in order to protect themselves and their communities.

Civilian involvement in civil wars is another trend that adults should be aware of, as non-combatants increasingly find themselves caught in the crossfire of conflicts. Understanding the role of civilians in civil wars and how to protect oneself in these situations is crucial for survival in modern conflicts.

Lastly, the role of private military companies in contemporary conflicts is a trend that has grown in recent years, with these organizations playing a significant role in conflict zones around the world. Adults must understand the implications of these private military companies and how to navigate their presence to survive and thrive in modern civil wars.

Chapter 2

Identifying Threats and Risks

Warning Signs of Potential Civil Conflict

Civil conflict is a grim reality that many societies face, and it is important to be aware of the warning signs that may indicate the onset of such a crisis.

In this subchapter, we will discuss some key indicators that could suggest a potential civil conflict is brewing in your area. By being vigilant and proactive, you can better prepare yourself and your loved ones for what may lie ahead.

One warning sign to watch out for is increasing political polarization and divisiveness within the population. When political rhetoric becomes increasingly hostile and inflammatory, it can create an environment ripe for conflict. Pay attention to how politicians and media outlets are framing issues and be wary of any attempts to dehumanize or demonize certain groups.

Another red flag to be aware of is the presence of armed groups or militias operating in your area. These groups may be fueled by extremist ideologies or grievances, and their presence can escalate tensions and lead to violence. Keep an eye out for any signs of militarization or paramilitary activity and report any suspicious behavior to the authorities.

Technological advancements in warfare have also changed the landscape of modern conflicts, with cyber warfare playing an increasingly prominent role. Be on the lookout for any signs of cyber-attacks or disruptions to critical infrastructure, as these could be precursors to a larger conflict.

Take steps to secure your own digital devices and data to minimize your vulnerability to cyber threats.

Civilian involvement in civil wars is another factor to consider when assessing the risk of conflict in your area. Pay attention to any signs of radicalization or recruitment efforts targeting vulnerable individuals and be cautious of any attempts to manipulate or exploit social divisions for political gain. Stay informed about local community dynamics and be prepared to intervene if you see signs of escalating tensions.

Lastly, keep an eye on the role of private military companies in contemporary conflicts. These organizations operate outside of traditional military structures and can have a significant impact on the course of a civil war.

Be aware of any signs of mercenary activity or foreign intervention in your area and take steps to protect yourself and your community from potential threats.

By staying informed and vigilant, you can better prepare yourself for the possibility of civil conflict and take steps to mitigate its impact on your life.

Key Players in Modern Civil Wars

In modern civil wars, some key players play a crucial role in the conflict and its outcome.

Understanding these key players is essential for anyone looking to navigate the complexities of civil war and prepare for potential conflicts. From government forces to rebel groups, each player brings their own set of tactics and strategies to the battlefield.

Government forces are typically the most well-equipped and organized players in a civil war.

They have access to resources and manpower, giving them a significant advantage over rebel groups. Government forces often rely on traditional military tactics and strategies, such as airstrikes and ground offensives, to maintain control and suppress rebel movements.

On the other hand, rebel groups are often characterized by their guerrilla warfare tactics and unconventional strategies. They may lack the resources and manpower of government forces, but they make up for it with their agility and ability to adapt to changing circumstances. Rebel groups often rely on hit-and-run tactics, ambushes, and sabotage to weaken government forces and gain support from the local population.

In addition to government forces and rebel groups, modern civil wars also involve a range of other key players, including private military companies, social media influencers, and cyber warfare experts. Private military companies are increasingly being used by governments and rebel groups to supplement their forces and carry out specialized operations.

Social media influencers can play a powerful role in shaping public opinion and mobilizing support for a particular cause.

Cyber warfare experts are also becoming increasingly important in modern civil wars, as conflicts are increasingly being fought online as well as on the battlefield.

Cyber-attacks can disrupt communication networks, sabotage infrastructure, and spread disinformation, making them a powerful tool for both government forces and rebel groups.

Understanding the role of these key players in modern civil wars is essential for anyone looking to prepare for potential conflicts and navigate the complex landscape of contemporary warfare.

Understanding the Impact of Foreign Involvement

Foreign involvement in modern civil wars is a key factor that can greatly impact the outcome of conflicts. It is essential for adults to be aware of the various ways in which foreign entities can influence and shape the course of a civil war.

Whether it is through military support, financial backing, or political alliances, foreign involvement can have far-reaching consequences on the outcome of a conflict.

One of the most significant impacts of foreign involvement in civil wars is the escalation of violence and the prolonging of conflicts. When external actors provide military support to one side of a conflict, it often leads to an increase in the intensity of fighting and can further destabilize the situation on the ground. This can result in more civilian casualties, displacement, and destruction of infrastructure, making it even more challenging for the conflict to be resolved peacefully.

Moreover, foreign involvement in civil wars can also exacerbate existing ethnic, religious, or political divides within a country. By taking sides in a conflict, external actors can deepen existing tensions and fuel animosities between different groups, making it harder for reconciliation and peacebuilding efforts to succeed. This can have long-lasting repercussions on the social fabric of a country and hinder efforts towards sustainable peace and stability.

In addition to military support, foreign entities can also leverage technological advancements in warfare to further their interests in a civil war.

From cyber warfare to the use of drones and unmanned aerial vehicles, foreign actors can gain a strategic advantage on the battlefield and gather valuable intelligence to support their allies. This can tip the balance of power in favor of one side and prolong the conflict even further.

Furthermore, the role of private military companies in contemporary conflicts cannot be overlooked. These non-state actors often operate in a grey area between legality and illegality, providing military services to governments, rebel groups, or other actors involved in a civil war.

Their presence can further complicate conflict dynamics and raise questions about accountability and transparency in modern warfare.

Overall, understanding the impact of foreign involvement in civil wars is crucial for adults who seek to navigate the complexities of modern conflicts. By being aware of the various ways in which external actors can influence and shape the course of a civil war, individuals can better prepare themselves for the challenges and risks associated with such conflicts. It is essential to stay informed, critically analyze sources of information, and advocate for peaceful and inclusive solutions to resolve civil wars and prevent further escalation of violence.

Chapter 3

Preparing for Urban Warfare

Urban Warfare Tactics and Strategies

In today's modern civil wars, urban warfare has become increasingly prevalent as conflicts move into densely populated areas. This subchapter will explore the tactics and strategies employed in urban warfare and how civilians can prepare for such scenarios.

One of the key tactics used in urban warfare is close-quarters combat, where fighting takes place within buildings, alleyways, and streets. This type of combat requires soldiers to be highly trained in room clearing, street fighting, and navigating tight spaces. It is crucial for civilians to understand the dangers of urban warfare and to have a plan in place for how to navigate and survive in these environments.

Technological advancements in warfare have also played a significant role in urban combat. From drones and unmanned aerial vehicles to advanced surveillance systems, modern warfare has become increasingly reliant on technology to gain an advantage in urban environments.

Understanding how these technologies are used and how to counter them is essential for both soldiers and civilians caught in urban warfare scenarios.

Cyber warfare has become another significant aspect of modern conflicts, with hackers and cyber terrorists targeting critical infrastructure and communication systems. The implications of cyber warfare in urban combat are vast, as entire cities can be brought to a standstill through cyber-attacks.

It is imperative for civilians to be aware of the potential for cyber warfare in urban conflicts and to take measures to protect themselves and their communities.

Civilian involvement in civil wars is also a key consideration in urban warfare.

Whether through resistance movements, humanitarian efforts, or simply trying to survive in a war-torn city, civilians play a crucial role in urban conflicts.

Understanding how to navigate these complex roles and how to protect oneself and one's family is essential for anyone living in a conflict zone.

In conclusion, urban warfare presents unique challenges and dangers in modern civil wars.

By understanding the tactics and strategies employed in urban combat, civilians can better prepare themselves for the realities of living in a war-torn city. From technological advancements to cyber warfare and civilian involvement, being informed and proactive is key to surviving and thriving in urban conflict zones.

Securing Your Home and Property in Urban Environments

In today's modern world, the threat of civil war is ever present, especially in urban environments where populations are dense and resources are limited. Securing your home and property in these environments is crucial to ensuring the safety of yourself and your loved ones.

From modern civil war tactics to technological advancements in warfare, there are many things to watch out for and prepare for in the event of a civil conflict.

One of the key strategies for securing your home in an urban environment is to fortify your property. This may include installing security cameras, reinforcing doors and windows, and creating a safe room to retreat to in case of an emergency. It is also important to have a plan in place for communication with your family and neighbors in the event of a civil war outbreak.

Technological advancements in warfare have made it easier for combatants to target civilians in urban areas. Drones and unmanned aerial vehicles are often used to gather intelligence and carry out attacks on civilian populations. Cyber warfare is another threat that can disrupt communication systems and infrastructure, making it difficult to coordinate a response to an emergency situation.

Civilian involvement in civil wars is a growing trend, with non-combatants often becoming targets for violence and exploitation.

It is important for individuals to be aware of their surroundings and to take precautions to protect themselves and their property. Psychological warfare and propaganda are commonly used tactics in modern conflicts, so it is important to be vigilant and not fall victim to misinformation.

Private military companies and social media also play a significant role in modern civil wars, with both being used to further the agendas of various factions. Environmental consequences of modern civil wars can be devastating, with infrastructure and resources being destroyed in the wake of conflict.

By understanding these threats and taking proactive measures to secure your home and property, you can increase your chances of surviving and thriving in a civil war situation.

Building a Survival Kit for Urban Conflicts

In the modern world, urban conflicts have become increasingly prevalent, posing unique challenges for civilians caught in the crossfire. Building a survival kit for urban conflicts is essential for anyone living in an area prone to civil unrest or conflict. This subchapter will explore the key items and strategies needed to navigate potentially dangerous situations.

One of the first items to include in your urban survival kit is a reliable communication device, such as a fully charged cell phone or a two-way radio. In urban conflicts, communication is key to staying informed and connected with loved ones. Additionally, having a map of the area and knowing multiple evacuation routes can help you navigate through the chaos and avoid dangerous areas.

Another crucial component of your survival kit should be first aid supplies, including bandages, antiseptic wipes, and any necessary medications. In urban conflicts, access to medical assistance may be limited, so being able to treat minor injuries on your own can be a lifesaver.

Additionally, having a flashlight, extra batteries, and a multi-tool can help you navigate dark or unfamiliar environments and address any unexpected challenges.

It is also important to include non-perishable food and water in your urban survival kit, as access to basic necessities may be compromised during a conflict. Pack enough supplies to last at least 72 hours, including high-energy snacks like granola bars and nuts. Having a water purification system or water purification tablets can also ensure you have access to clean drinking water in emergency situations.

Lastly, consider including items for self-defense in your urban survival kit, such as pepper spray, a whistle, or a small pocketknife. While it is important to prioritize de-escalation and conflict avoidance, having these tools can provide an added layer of security in dangerous situations.

Remember to familiarize yourself with local laws regarding self-defense and use these items responsibly. By building a comprehensive survival kit for urban conflicts, you can better prepare yourself for the challenges of modern civil unrest and increase your chances of staying safe in uncertain times.

Chapter 4
Embracing Technological Advancements

The Role of Technology in Modern Warfare

The demon appeared inside the dimension that held those imprisoned by the Truth Dreamers. For many years many were cast into this void to be trapped for eternity.

As modern warfare continues to evolve, technology plays an increasingly crucial role in shaping the dynamics of conflicts around the world. From advancements in weaponry to the utilization of cyber warfare tactics, technology has fundamentally transformed the way wars are fought and won.

In this subchapter, we will explore the various ways in which technology influences modern warfare and how civilians can prepare themselves for the challenges ahead.

One of the most significant technological advancements in modern warfare is the development of unmanned aerial vehicles, commonly known as drones.

These remote-controlled aircraft have revolutionized reconnaissance and precision strike capabilities, allowing military forces to gather intelligence and conduct targeted strikes with unprecedented accuracy.

However, the use of drones also raises ethical concerns regarding civilian casualties and the erosion of traditional rules of engagement.

In addition to drones, cyber warfare has emerged as a potent tool in the arsenal of modern militaries. Hackers can infiltrate enemy networks, disrupt communications, and sabotage critical infrastructure without ever firing a single shot.

The implications of cyber warfare in modern conflicts are vast, as nations must now defend against virtual attacks that can have real-world consequences on the battlefield.

Furthermore, the role of private military companies (PMCs) has grown in contemporary conflicts, with these organizations providing specialized services ranging from logistics support to combat operations. While PMCs offer flexibility and expertise, their involvement in conflicts blurs the lines between state and non-state actors, raising questions about accountability and the ethics of outsourcing military functions to private entities.

As technology continues to shape the landscape of modern warfare, civilians must be aware of the potential environmental consequences of conflicts, such as the destruction of ecosystems and contamination of water sources.

Understanding the interconnected nature of warfare and the environment is crucial for preparing for the long-term impacts of civil wars on communities and ecosystems alike.

In conclusion, the role of technology in modern warfare is undeniable, with advancements in weaponry, cyber capabilities, and unmanned aerial vehicles reshaping the way conflicts are fought and won.

By staying informed and prepared for the challenges ahead, civilians can navigate the complexities of modern civil wars and mitigate the risks associated with evolving technologies on the battlefield.

Utilizing Surveillance and Communication Tools

In the modern age, surveillance and communication tools play a crucial role in both warfare and civilian life. For those preparing for the possibility of civil war, understanding how to utilize these tools can mean the difference between life and death.

From monitoring enemy movements to communicating with allies, surveillance, and communication tools are essential for staying one step ahead in a conflict.

Urban warfare tactics and strategies have evolved with the advancement of technology, making it more important than ever to have access to surveillance tools such as drones and unmanned aerial vehicles. These tools can provide valuable intel on enemy positions, allowing for more strategic and precise attacks. Additionally, communication tools such as encrypted messaging apps can help ensure that sensitive information remains secure.

Technological advancements in warfare have led to the rise of cyber warfare, which poses a significant threat in modern conflicts.

Understanding how to protect against cyber-attacks and secure communication channels is essential for anyone involved in a civil war scenario. By utilizing encryption and other security measures, individuals can minimize the risk of being compromised by cyber threats.

Civilian involvement in civil wars is becoming increasingly common, with non-combatants often caught in the crossfire. By utilizing surveillance tools to monitor enemy movements and communication tools to coordinate with other civilians, individuals can better protect themselves and their communities.

Additionally, understanding psychological warfare and propaganda tactics can help civilians discern fact from fiction in a conflict zone.

The use of drones and unmanned aerial vehicles has revolutionized modern warfare, allowing for more precise and efficient attacks. However, these tools also have environmental consequences, such as the destruction of infrastructure and the displacement of civilians.

By understanding the impact of these technologies, individuals can better prepare for the environmental consequences of modern civil wars.

Additionally, the role of private military companies in contemporary conflicts raises ethical concerns, highlighting the need for transparency and accountability in warfare.

Benefits and Drawbacks of Technological Warfare

In the modern age, warfare has evolved to include a significant technological component. While technological advancements have brought about new methods of combat and increased efficiency on the battlefield, they also come with their own set of benefits and drawbacks.

One of the main benefits of technological warfare is the ability to target enemies with precision.

With advancements in drone technology and unmanned aerial vehicles, military forces can now strike with accuracy and minimal collateral damage. This can help to reduce civilian casualties and limit the destruction of infrastructure in conflict zones.

Additionally, technological warfare allows for greater surveillance and intelligence-gathering capabilities. This can give military forces a strategic advantage by providing real-time information on enemy movements and intentions. By utilizing cyber warfare tactics, governments can also disrupt enemy communications and sabotage their infrastructure without the need for physical combat.

However, there are also drawbacks to relying heavily on technology in warfare. One major concern is the potential for cyber-attacks and hacking, which can cripple military systems and compromise sensitive information. In addition, the use of drones and unmanned aerial vehicles raises ethical questions about the morality of remote-controlled warfare and the psychological impact on those operating the technology.

Furthermore, the environmental consequences of modern civil wars must be considered.

Technological warfare often involves the use of chemical weapons, explosives, and other harmful substances that can have long-lasting effects on the environment and local populations. This can lead to widespread pollution, deforestation, and destruction of natural habitats in conflict zones.

Overall, while technological warfare offers many benefits in terms of precision, surveillance, and intelligence gathering, it also comes with significant drawbacks that must be carefully weighed. As conflicts continue to evolve in the modern age, it is important for military forces and policymakers to consider the implications of relying too heavily on technology in warfare and to find a balance that minimizes harm to civilians and the environment.

Chapter 5

Navigating Cyber Warfare

Understanding Cyber Attacks and Defenses

In today's modern world, cyber-attacks have become a major threat in conflicts and civil wars.

Understanding how these attacks work and how to defend against them is crucial for survival in the digital age. Cyber-attacks can range from simple phishing scams to sophisticated hacking operations that can disrupt entire systems and infrastructure.

In the context of modern civil wars, cyber-attacks have become a powerful tool for both state and non-state actors to gain an advantage over their enemies.

One of the key aspects of understanding cyber-attacks is knowing how to defend against them. This involves implementing strong cybersecurity measures, such as using encryption, multi-factor authentication, and regularly updating software to patch vulnerabilities. It also requires vigilance and awareness of potential threats, such as suspicious emails or links that could be phishing attempts. By taking proactive steps to protect digital assets, individuals and organizations can mitigate the risk of falling victim to cyber-attacks in a modern civil war scenario.

In addition to defending against cyber-attacks, it is important to understand the implications of these attacks in modern conflicts. Cyber warfare can have far-reaching consequences, including disrupting critical infrastructure, stealing sensitive information, and spreading misinformation to manipulate public opinion.

In the context of a civil war, cyber-attacks can be used to target civilians, disrupt supply chains, and undermine the legitimacy of the government or opposing factions. By understanding the potential impacts of cyber warfare, individuals can better prepare for and respond to these threats in a modern civil war environment.

As civilians become increasingly involved in modern civil wars, the risk of being caught in the crossfire of cyber-attacks also grows. It is important for individuals to be aware of the risks and take steps to protect themselves and their families from potential harm.

This includes staying informed about the latest cyber threats, educating themselves on best practices for cybersecurity, and being cautious when sharing personal information online. By taking proactive steps to safeguard their digital lives, individuals can reduce their vulnerability to cyber-attacks in a modern civil war situation.

In conclusion, understanding cyber-attacks and defenses is essential for survival in the digital age, especially in the context of modern civil wars.

By implementing strong cybersecurity measures, being aware of potential threats, and understanding the implications of cyber warfare, individuals can better protect themselves and their communities from the devastating effects of cyber-attacks.

In a world where technology plays an increasingly important role in conflicts, being prepared for cyber threats is crucial for ensuring safety and security in modern civil wars.

Cyber Warfare's Influence on Civil Conflicts

Cyber warfare has become a key player in modern civil conflicts, influencing the way wars are fought and won. From hacking into enemy networks to spreading disinformation and propaganda online, cyber warfare has the power to disrupt entire nations and shift the balance of power in a conflict.

In today's digital age, understanding the implications of cyber warfare is crucial for anyone preparing to navigate the complexities of a civil war.

As civil conflicts increasingly move from traditional battlegrounds to urban environments, the use of cyber warfare tactics becomes even more prevalent.

Urban warfare presents unique challenges for both military forces and civilians, as the dense population centers provide ample opportunities for cyber-attacks and propaganda campaigns to sow chaos and confusion.

Understanding how cyber warfare is used in urban environments is essential for anyone looking to survive and thrive in a modern civil war.

Technological advancements in warfare have also paved the way for new forms of cyber warfare, including the use of drones and unmanned aerial vehicles (UAVs) to conduct surveillance and targeted strikes. These technologies can be used to gather intelligence, carry out assassinations, and deliver supplies to rebel groups, all while remaining virtually undetectable.

As civilians caught in the crossfire of civil conflicts, it is important to be aware of how these technologies are being used and how they may impact your safety and security.

One of the most insidious aspects of cyber warfare is the way it can be used to manipulate public opinion and shape the narrative of a conflict.

Psychological warfare and propaganda play a crucial role in modern civil wars, with social media platforms being used to spread false information and sow discord among the population. Understanding how propaganda is used in civil conflicts can help individuals discern fact from fiction and make informed decisions about their safety and well-being.

In the face of these challenges, it is important for individuals to be proactive in preparing for the potential impacts of cyber warfare on civil conflicts. From safeguarding personal data and communications to being vigilant against online threats, there are steps that can be taken to mitigate the risks of cyber-attacks during times of conflict. By staying informed and educated about the implications of cyber warfare on civil conflicts, individuals can better protect themselves and their communities in an increasingly digital battlefield.

Protecting Your Digital Assets in Times of War

In times of war, it is crucial to not only protect physical assets but also digital assets. As technology continues to advance, so does the risk of cyber warfare. Hackers can target individuals, businesses, and even governments, creating chaos and confusion during conflict. To protect your digital assets in times of war, it is important to take proactive measures to secure your information.

One way to protect your digital assets is to regularly update your security software and use strong passwords. Hackers often exploit outdated software and weak passwords to gain access to sensitive information. By staying vigilant and keeping your defenses up to date, you can reduce the risk of a cyber-attack compromising your digital assets.

Another important step in protecting your digital assets is to back up your data regularly. In the event of a cyber-attack or other digital threat, having backups of your important information can help you recover quickly and minimize the impact on your operations. Cloud storage, external hard drives, and other backup solutions can help ensure that your data remains safe and accessible.

It is also important to be cautious when sharing information online during times of war. Social media and other digital platforms can be used by malicious actors to spread misinformation and propaganda. By being mindful of what you share and who you interact with online, you can help protect your digital assets and avoid falling victim to cyber warfare tactics.

By taking these steps to protect your digital assets in times of war, you can help safeguard your information and maintain your security in an increasingly digital world. Stay informed, stay vigilant, and stay prepared to defend yourself against cyber threats during times of conflict.

Chapter 6

Engaging Civilians in Conflict

The Importance of Civilian Participation in Civil Wars

Civil wars are complex and devastating conflicts that can have long-lasting effects on a country and its people. In modern civil wars, civilians often find themselves caught in the crossfire, facing violence, displacement, and loss. However, civilian participation in civil wars can play a crucial role in shaping the outcome of the conflict.

One of the key reasons why civilian participation is important in civil wars is that civilians are often the ones most directly affected by the conflict. They are the ones who face the daily reality of violence and instability, and their voices and experiences can provide valuable insights into the root causes of the conflict and potential solutions.

By actively participating in the peace process and advocating for their rights, civilians can help shape a more inclusive and sustainable peace agreement.

Furthermore, civilian involvement in civil wars can help to hold warring parties accountable for their actions. By documenting human rights abuses, providing support to victims, and advocating for justice, civilians can help to ensure that perpetrators are held accountable for their crimes.

This can help to deter future violations and contribute to a more just and peaceful society.

In addition, civilian participation in civil wars can help to build resilience and strengthen communities in the face of conflict. By organizing grassroots initiatives, providing humanitarian assistance, and promoting social cohesion, civilians can help to mitigate the impact of the conflict and build a foundation for recovery and reconciliation.

This can help to build a more resilient society that is better equipped to withstand future challenges.

Overall, civilian participation in civil wars is essential for building a more inclusive, just, and sustainable peace. By actively engaging in the peace process, advocating for their rights, and holding perpetrators accountable, civilians can help to shape a more peaceful and prosperous future for their country.

It is important for adults to be aware of the crucial role that civilian participation plays in civil wars and to support and empower civilians in their efforts to build a better future for themselves and their communities.

Ways to Support or Resist Warring Factions

During a modern civil war, it can be difficult to navigate the complex web of warring factions and choose a side to support or resist. However, there are several ways in which individuals can act to either support or resist these factions and play a role in shaping the outcome of the conflict.

One way to support warring factions is through providing financial assistance or resources. This can help to bolster the strength of a particular faction and give them the resources they need to carry out their objectives.

However, it is important to carefully consider the implications of providing support to a particular faction, as this could have unintended consequences and prolong the conflict.

On the other hand, individuals can also choose to resist warring factions by refusing to provide support or resources to any side. This can help to prevent the escalation of the conflict and promote peaceful resolution.

Additionally, individuals can also choose to speak out against the violence and atrocities committed by warring factions, raising awareness, and calling for accountability.

Another way to support or resist warring factions is through engaging in humanitarian efforts. This can involve providing aid to civilians affected by the conflict, advocating for human rights and international law, and working towards peacebuilding and reconciliation.

By supporting humanitarian efforts, individuals can help to alleviate the suffering caused by the conflict and promote a more peaceful resolution.

Ultimately, whether choosing to support or resist warring factions, it is important for individuals to carefully consider the potential consequences of their actions and work towards promoting peace and stability.

By taking a stand and actively participating in efforts to support or resist warring factions, individuals can play a crucial role in shaping the outcome of a modern civil war and working towards a more peaceful future.

Ensuring Civilian Safety Amidst Conflict

In times of conflict, ensuring civilian safety is paramount. As modern warfare continues to evolve, civilians are increasingly becoming targets in conflicts around the world. From urban warfare tactics to technological advancements in warfare, civilians must be aware of the potential dangers they face and take necessary precautions to protect themselves and their loved ones.

Urban warfare poses a unique set of challenges for civilians caught in the crossfire. With fighting often taking place in densely populated areas, civilians must be vigilant and prepared to evacuate at a moment's notice. It is crucial to have a plan in place for escaping dangerous situations and knowing where nearby shelters or safe zones are located.

Technological advancements in warfare have also changed the landscape of conflict, with drones and unmanned aerial vehicles becoming increasingly prevalent on the battlefield. Civilians must be aware of the potential dangers posed by these weapons and take steps to protect themselves from potential attacks. This may include staying indoors during drone strikes or seeking shelter in underground bunkers.

Cyber warfare is another growing threat in modern conflicts, with hackers targeting critical infrastructure and disrupting communications networks. Civilians must be vigilant about protecting their personal information and be cautious of phishing scams and other cyber threats. It is also important to have backup communication plans in place in case traditional communication channels are disrupted.

In addition to physical threats, civilians must also be aware of the psychological warfare and propaganda tactics used in modern conflicts.

The news media and propaganda can be used to manipulate public opinion and turn civilians against one another. It is important to critically evaluate information and be aware of potential misinformation campaigns. By staying informed and vigilant, civilians can better protect themselves and their communities in times of conflict.

Chapter 7
Psychological Warfare and Propaganda

Impact of Psychological Tactics in Modern Conflicts

In modern conflicts, psychological tactics play a crucial role in shaping the outcomes of battles and wars. The impact of psychological warfare on the battlefield cannot be underestimated, as it can influence the morale and behavior of both soldiers and civilians. By understanding how psychological tactics are used in modern conflicts, individuals can better prepare themselves for the challenges of urban warfare and other forms of contemporary conflict.

One key aspect of psychological tactics in modern conflicts is the use of propaganda to manipulate public opinion and sway perceptions of the enemy.

Propaganda can be disseminated through various mediums, including social media, traditional media outlets, and even word of mouth.

By spreading misinformation and disinformation, warring factions can create confusion and fear among the civilian population, making it easier to control and manipulate them.

Another important psychological tactic in modern conflicts is the use of fear and intimidation to control territory and populations. By instilling fear in civilians through acts of violence and brutality, warring factions can assert their dominance and maintain control over key strategic locations.

This tactic is often used in urban warfare, where civilians are caught in the crossfire and become pawns in the larger conflict.

Technological advancements in warfare have also played a significant role in the evolution of psychological tactics on the battlefield. The use of drones and unmanned aerial vehicles (UAVs) has revolutionized the way wars are fought, allowing for precision strikes and surveillance capabilities that were previously unimaginable.

By leveraging these technologies, warring factions can project power and dominance over their enemies, instilling fear, and uncertainty in their ranks.

Cyber warfare is another area where psychological tactics are increasingly being utilized in modern conflicts. By targeting critical infrastructure, communications networks, and government systems, cyber attackers can disrupt the enemy's ability to wage war and sow confusion and chaos among their ranks. This form of warfare is particularly insidious, as it can be carried out anonymously and with minimal risk of retaliation.

Overall, the impact of psychological tactics in modern conflicts cannot be overstated. By understanding how these tactics are used and the ways in which they can influence the outcome of battles and wars, individuals can better prepare themselves for the challenges of contemporary conflict.

Whether it be through propaganda, fear and intimidation, technological advancements, or cyber warfare, psychological tactics will continue to shape the future of warfare and conflict in the 21st century.

Identifying Propaganda Techniques

In the chaotic landscape of modern civil wars, propaganda has become a powerful tool used to manipulate public opinion and sow discord among opposing factions.

By understanding the various techniques employed in propaganda, individuals can better equip themselves to discern fact from fiction and safeguard against being misled.

One common propaganda technique is the use of loaded language, which involves the use of emotionally charged words to evoke a specific response from the audience. For example, labeling an opposing faction as "terrorists" can sway public opinion against them without providing any concrete evidence of their actions.

By recognizing loaded language and questioning the motives behind it, individuals can avoid falling victim to propaganda tactics.

Another propaganda technique to watch out for is bandwagon propaganda, which plays on the human desire to conform to popular opinion.

By portraying a certain belief or action as widely accepted, propagandists can pressure individuals into adopting the same stance without critically evaluating the information presented. It is crucial for individuals to resist the urge to follow the crowd blindly and instead engage in independent research to form their own opinions.

Fear-mongering is a particularly insidious propaganda technique that preys on people's anxieties and insecurities. By exaggerating threats and creating a sense of imminent danger, propagandists can manipulate individuals into supporting extreme measures or ideologies. It is important for individuals to remain vigilant and question the validity of fear-based propaganda to avoid being manipulated by those seeking to exploit their emotions.

In the digital age, propaganda has taken on new forms through the use of social media and online platforms. The dissemination of misinformation and fake news has become rampant, making it increasingly difficult to discern truth from falsehood.

By developing critical thinking skills and verifying sources before sharing information, individuals can help combat the spread of propaganda and contribute to a more informed public discourse. By staying informed and vigilant, individuals can protect themselves against the insidious tactics of propaganda and play a proactive role in promoting truth and transparency during modern civil conflicts.

Maintaining Mental Resilience in War Zones

In the midst of modern civil wars, one of the most crucial aspects of survival is maintaining mental resilience. The constant threat of violence, destruction, and loss can take a toll on even the strongest individuals. It is essential for adults in war zones to prioritize their mental well-being in order to navigate the challenges they face on a daily basis.

Urban warfare tactics and strategies have become increasingly prevalent in modern conflicts, making it even more important for individuals to stay mentally sharp and adaptable. The chaotic and unpredictable nature of urban warfare can be overwhelming, but by maintaining mental resilience, individuals can better handle the challenges they encounter in these environments.

Technological advancements in warfare have revolutionized the way conflicts are fought, presenting new challenges for those caught during civil wars. From cyber warfare to the use of drones and unmanned aerial vehicles, the modern battlefield is constantly evolving. By staying mentally resilient, individuals can better cope with the complexities of these technological advancements and adapt to the changing landscape of warfare.

Civilian involvement in civil wars is another important factor to consider when discussing mental resilience in war zones. Whether individuals are directly involved in the conflict or simply caught in the crossfire, the psychological impact of civil war can be profound. By prioritizing mental well-being and seeking support when needed, adults can better navigate the challenges they face in these turbulent times.

In conclusion, maintaining mental resilience in war zones is essential for adults facing the challenges of modern civil wars. By staying mentally sharp, adaptable, and seeking support when needed, individuals can better cope with the chaos and uncertainty of conflict. In the face of urban warfare tactics, technological advancements, and civilian involvement, mental resilience is a crucial tool for survival in the modern battlefield.

Chapter 8

Utilizing Drones and UAVs

The Rise of Unmanned Aerial Vehicles in Warfare

In recent years, the use of unmanned aerial vehicles (UAVs) in warfare has become increasingly prevalent. These drones, equipped with cameras and sometimes weapons, have revolutionized the way conflicts are fought and have quickly become a staple in modern warfare.

The rise of UAVs has had a significant impact on the strategies and tactics used in urban warfare, as they provide a unique vantage point and the ability to strike targets with precision.

Technological advancements in warfare have played a key role in the development and proliferation of UAVs. These drones are now capable of flying longer distances, staying in the air for extended periods of time, and carrying out complex missions with minimal human intervention. As a result, they have become a valuable tool for military forces looking to gain an edge in modern conflicts.

One of the most concerning aspects of the use of UAVs in warfare is the potential for cyber warfare and its implications. As drones become more interconnected and reliant on digital systems, they become vulnerable to hacking and cyber-attacks. This could lead to disastrous consequences if hostile actors were able to take control of these drones and use them against their intended targets.

Civilian involvement in civil wars has also been impacted by the rise of UAVs. In some conflicts, non-state actors have been able to acquire and operate drones, using them to gather intelligence, conduct surveillance, and even carry out attacks. This blurring of the lines between military and civilian use of drones has raised ethical and legal questions about their use in warfare.

The use of drones and UAVs in warfare has not only had immediate tactical implications but also environmental consequences. The increased use of drones has led to concerns about the impact on the environment, as these aircraft emit greenhouse gases and contribute to air pollution.

Additionally, the use of drones in conflict zones has raised questions about the long-term effects on ecosystems and wildlife. As the use of UAVs continues to grow, it is essential for policymakers and military leaders to consider the environmental impact of these technologies in their decision-making processes.

Drones' Role in Surveillance and Combat Operations

Drones have become an integral part of modern warfare, playing a crucial role in surveillance and combat operations.

These unmanned aerial vehicles have revolutionized the way military forces gather intelligence and conduct targeted strikes on enemy targets. In the context of civil wars, drones have proven to be invaluable assets for both government forces and rebel groups.

In terms of surveillance, drones provide real-time information on enemy movements, fortifications, and supply routes. This data allows military commanders to make informed decisions about their next course of action, minimizing the risk to their troops. Drones can also be used to monitor civilian populations, identify potential threats, and gather evidence of war crimes.

When it comes to combat operations, drones can carry out precision strikes on enemy targets with minimal collateral damage. Armed drones, also known as unmanned combat aerial vehicles (UCAVs), can be equipped with missiles, bombs, and other weapons to neutralize high-value targets such as enemy leaders, weapons caches, and communication centers. This capability has significantly changed the dynamics of modern warfare, allowing for more efficient and effective military operations.

However, the use of drones in civil wars has raised ethical concerns about civilian casualties and violations of international law. Critics argue that the indiscriminate use of drones in populated areas can lead to unintended harm to non-combatants, undermining efforts to win hearts and minds.

Furthermore, the proliferation of drones among non-state actors has made it difficult to hold perpetrators of drone attacks accountable for their actions.

As technology continues to advance, drones are likely to play an even greater role in future conflicts, including civil wars. It is crucial for military forces and policymakers to carefully consider the ethical implications of drone warfare and ensure that their use is in line with international humanitarian law.

By understanding the capabilities and limitations of drones, civilians can better prepare for the potential impact of these unmanned aerial vehicles on modern civil wars.

Ethical Considerations of Drone Warfare

In recent years, drone warfare has become a prominent topic of discussion in modern conflicts. The use of drones and unmanned aerial vehicles (UAVs) in warfare has raised several ethical considerations that must be taken into account.

In this subchapter, we will explore some of the key ethical considerations of drone warfare and how they impact the modern civil war landscape.

One of the primary ethical concerns surrounding drone warfare is the issue of civilian casualties.

While drones can target specific individuals with precision, there is still a risk of collateral damage to innocent civilians. This raises questions about the moral responsibility of those who deploy drones and the potential consequences of their actions on civilian populations.

Another ethical consideration of drone warfare is the potential for remote operators to become desensitized to the act of killing. Unlike traditional warfare, where soldiers are physically present on the battlefield, drone operators can carry out strikes from thousands of miles away.

This raises concerns about the psychological impact of remote warfare and the implications it may have on the mental health of those involved.

Additionally, there is a concern about the lack of transparency and accountability in drone warfare. With the ability to carry out strikes covertly and without the need for boots on the ground, it can be difficult to hold those responsible for drone attacks to account. This raises questions about the legality of drone warfare and the need for greater oversight and regulation.

Furthermore, the use of drones in warfare raises broader ethical questions about the nature of modern conflict. As technology continues to advance, the line between combatant and civilian becomes increasingly blurred. This challenges traditional notions of warfare and raises questions about the morality of using advanced technology to carry out military operations.

Overall, the ethical considerations of drone warfare are complex and multifaceted. As modern civil wars continue to evolve, it is essential for policymakers, military leaders, and the public to carefully consider the ethical implications of using drones in warfare and to strive for a more ethical and humane approach to conflict resolution.

Chapter 9

Addressing Environmental Consequences

Environmental Destruction in Modern Civil Wars

One of the often-overlooked consequences of modern civil wars is the environmental destruction that occurs because of the conflict. In the chaos of war, natural resources are often exploited, and ecosystems are devastated, leading to long-term environmental damage. This destruction can have far-reaching consequences for both the environment and the people living in war-torn regions.

Urban warfare tactics and strategies play a significant role in causing environmental destruction during modern civil wars. The use of heavy artillery, explosives, and chemical weapons in densely populated urban areas can lead to widespread pollution and destruction of buildings and infrastructure. The indiscriminate targeting of civilian populations further exacerbates the environmental impact of urban warfare.

Technological advancements in warfare have also contributed to environmental destruction in modern civil wars. The use of drones and unmanned aerial vehicles (UAVs) has made it easier for warring factions to carry out targeted attacks on specific locations, leading to increased environmental damage.

Additionally, the widespread use of heavy machinery and vehicles in conflict zones has resulted in deforestation, soil erosion, and pollution of water sources.

Cyber warfare is another aspect of modern conflicts that has environmental implications.

The use of cyber-attacks to disrupt critical infrastructure, such as power plants and water treatment facilities, can lead to environmental disasters and further exacerbate the impact of civil wars on the environment.

The interconnected nature of modern technology means that a cyber-attack in one area can have far-reaching consequences for the environment.

Civilian involvement in civil wars also plays a role in environmental destruction.

Displaced populations often resort to unsustainable practices, such as deforestation for fuel or poaching for food, to survive in war-torn regions.

This further degrades the environment and exacerbates the environmental impact of modern civil wars.

Governments and international organizations must address the environmental consequences of civil wars and work towards sustainable solutions to protect the environment and the people living in conflict zones.

Mitigating Ecological Impacts of Conflict

In times of conflict, the ecological impacts can often be overlooked as the focus is primarily on the human cost of war. However, it is important to recognize that the environment also suffers greatly during periods of civil unrest and warfare.

In this subchapter, we will discuss ways in which we can mitigate the ecological impacts of conflict and preserve our natural resources for future generations.

One of the most significant ecological impacts of conflict is the destruction of natural habitats and ecosystems.

Urban warfare tactics and strategies often involve the bombing of buildings and infrastructure, which can result in the loss of wildlife and vegetation.

To mitigate this impact, it is important to prioritize the protection of natural areas and implement measures to prevent further destruction.

Technological advancements in warfare have also had a detrimental impact on the environment. The use of drones and unmanned aerial vehicles in warfare can result in the contamination of air, water, and soil due to the chemicals and fuels used in these machines.

By developing more sustainable technologies and reducing our reliance on harmful substances, we can lessen the environmental consequences of modern civil wars.

Another important aspect to consider is the role of private military companies in contemporary conflicts. These organizations often operate with little oversight and can cause significant environmental damage in their pursuit of profit.

By holding these companies accountable for their actions and ensuring that they adhere to strict environmental regulations, we can minimize their negative impact on the environment.

Civilian involvement in civil wars can also have a profound effect on the environment. Displaced populations often resort to illegal logging, poaching, and other destructive activities to survive. By providing support and resources to these communities, we can help prevent further degradation of the environment and promote sustainable practices.

In conclusion, it is crucial that we take proactive measures to mitigate the ecological impacts of conflict. By prioritizing the protection of natural habitats, promoting sustainable technologies, holding private military companies accountable, and supporting displaced populations, we can help preserve our environment in the face of modern civil wars.

It is up to us to act and ensure that future generations have access to a healthy and thriving planet.

Preparing for Environmental Disasters During War

Environmental disasters during war can be devastating and have long-lasting effects on the environment and the population. As such, it is crucial for individuals to be prepared for such scenarios to increase their chances of survival. In this subchapter, we will discuss some key strategies for preparing for environmental disasters during war.

One important aspect to consider when preparing for environmental disasters during war is to have a well-stocked emergency kit. This kit should include essential items such as food, water, first aid supplies, and tools for shelter and communication. Having these items readily available can make a significant difference in the event of a disaster.

In addition to having an emergency kit, it is also important to have a plan in place for evacuation and shelter. Knowing where to go and how to get there quickly and safely can be critical in a high-stress situation. It is also important to have a communication plan in place so that you can stay in contact with loved ones and emergency services during a disaster.

Another important aspect of preparing for environmental disasters during a war is to be aware of potential hazards in your environment. This includes being mindful of things like contaminated water sources, hazardous materials, and unstable structures. By being aware of these risks, you can take steps to avoid them and stay safe during a disaster.

Finally, it is important to stay informed about potential environmental disasters and how they may impact on your area. This includes keeping up to date with news and alerts from local authorities, as well as staying informed about potential threats from the conflict itself. By staying informed and prepared, you can increase your chances of surviving and thriving in the face of environmental disasters during war.

Chapter 10

Private Military Companies in Warfare

The Proliferation of PMCs in Contemporary Conflicts

Private Military Companies (PMCs) have become increasingly prevalent in modern civil wars, playing a significant role in the dynamics of conflict. These companies, often operating outside of traditional military structures, offer a range of services including security, logistics, and training to governments, rebel groups, and other actors involved in conflict.

The use of PMCs has raised concerns about accountability, transparency, and the potential for human rights abuses in conflict zones.

One of the key reasons for the proliferation of PMCs in contemporary conflicts is the outsourcing of military functions by governments seeking cost-effective solutions to combat insurgency and terrorism.

PMCs offer a flexible and efficient alternative to traditional military forces, allowing governments to deploy specialized personnel and resources quickly and without the bureaucratic constraints of conventional military operations.

However, the use of PMCs also raises ethical questions about the privatization of warfare and the potential for profit-driven motivations to influence decision-making in conflict zones.

PMCs have also played a role in urban warfare tactics and strategies, where their specialized training and equipment have been utilized in complex and densely populated environments. The use of PMCs in urban warfare has raised concerns about civilian casualties, collateral damage, and the impact of private actors on the dynamics of conflict.

Additionally, the involvement of PMCs in urban warfare has blurred the lines between military and civilian actors, complicating efforts to protect non-combatants and uphold international humanitarian law.

Technological advancements in warfare have further enabled the proliferation of PMCs in contemporary conflicts, as these companies have access to cutting-edge equipment, surveillance technology, and weapons systems. The use of drones and unmanned aerial vehicles by PMCs has revolutionized the way conflicts are fought, allowing for precision strikes, reconnaissance, and intelligence gathering in real time.

However, the use of technology by PMCs also raises concerns about the ethical and legal implications of autonomous weapons systems and the potential for indiscriminate targeting of civilians.

The role of PMCs in contemporary conflicts highlights the evolving nature of warfare and the challenges posed by the privatization of military functions.

As PMCs continue to play a significant role in conflict zones around the world, governments, international organizations, and civil society need to engage in dialogue and regulation to ensure accountability, transparency, and respect for human rights in conflict situations.

The proliferation of PMCs underscores the need for a comprehensive approach to modern civil war survival that addresses the complex interplay of military, technological, and ethical considerations in conflict resolution.

Understanding the Role of Mercenaries in Civil Wars

In the chaotic landscape of modern civil wars, mercenaries play a significant and often controversial role. Understanding their involvement in conflicts is crucial for anyone seeking to navigate the dangers of urban warfare and prepare for the worst-case scenarios.

Mercenaries, also known as private military companies, are hired guns who operate outside of traditional military structures.

They are often employed by governments, rebel groups, or even corporations to carry out specialized tasks in conflict zones.

One of the key reasons mercenaries are sought after in civil wars is their specialized skills and training.

Unlike regular military forces, mercenaries are often highly skilled and experienced in urban warfare tactics and strategies. They can provide valuable expertise in areas such as counterinsurgency, intelligence gathering, and close-quarters combat. Their presence can tip the scales in favor of their employers, but they can also exacerbate conflicts by fueling violence and instability.

Technological advancements in warfare have also transformed the role of mercenaries in civil wars. With the rise of drones and unmanned aerial vehicles, mercenaries can now carry out surveillance, reconnaissance, and even targeted strikes with unprecedented precision. This has raised ethical concerns about the use of force in conflicts, as well as the potential for civilian casualties.

Cyber warfare has further blurred the lines between traditional and non-traditional actors in modern conflicts, with mercenaries playing a key role in conducting cyber-attacks and information operations.

The involvement of private military companies in contemporary conflicts has raised questions about the accountability and legality of their actions. While mercenaries are often subject to international laws and conventions, they operate in a legal gray zone that allows them to evade prosecution for war crimes and human rights abuses.

This has led to calls for greater regulation and oversight of the private military industry, to ensure that their actions are in line with international norms and standards.

In conclusion, understanding the role of mercenaries in civil wars is essential for anyone seeking to navigate the dangers of modern conflicts. By being aware of their capabilities, motivations, and limitations, individuals can better prepare for the challenges of urban warfare and protect themselves and their loved ones. It is crucial to stay informed about the evolving nature of warfare and the ways in which mercenaries are shaping the course of modern conflicts. By staying vigilant and proactive, we can mitigate the risks and uncertainties of civil wars and work towards building a more peaceful and secure world.

Legal and Ethical Issues Surrounding Private Militaries

Private militaries, also known as private military companies (PMCs), have become increasingly prevalent in modern conflicts around the world. These organizations, hired by governments or private entities to provide security and military services, raise several legal and ethical concerns. One of the main issues surrounding PMCs is the lack of accountability and oversight compared to traditional military forces. This can lead to situations where private military personnel operate with impunity, potentially violating human rights and international laws.

From a legal perspective, the use of private militaries raises questions about who is responsible for the actions of these companies. In cases where private military personnel commit crimes or human rights abuses, it can be difficult to hold anyone accountable due to the complex web of contracts and agreements that govern their operations. Additionally, the use of PMCs blurs the line between military and civilian actors, making it unclear which laws and regulations apply to them.

Ethically, the use of private militaries raises concerns about the motivations behind their involvement in conflicts. While some argue that PMCs provide a valuable service by filling gaps in military capabilities, others worry that these companies are driven by profit rather than principles. This can lead to situations where private military personnel prioritize their own interests over those of the people they are supposed to be protecting.

Another ethical issue surrounding private militaries is the potential for conflicts of interest. Because PMCs are often employed by private entities or individuals, there is a risk that their actions could be influenced by factors other than military necessity. This can lead to situations where private military personnel engage in activities that serve the interests of their employers rather than the greater good.

Overall, the use of private militaries in modern conflicts raises complex legal and ethical issues that require careful consideration. As the role of PMCs continues to grow, it is important for governments, international organizations, and civil society to address these concerns and ensure that private military companies operate in a manner that is consistent with international law and human rights standards.

Chapter 11

Impact of Social Media on Civil Wars

Social Media's Influence on Conflict Narratives

Social media has become an integral part of our daily lives, shaping the way we communicate, consume information, and even perceive reality. In the context of modern civil wars, social media plays a pivotal role in shaping conflict narratives and influencing public opinion.

The instantaneous nature of platforms like Twitter, Facebook, and Instagram allows for the rapid dissemination of information, often blurring the line between fact and fiction.

One of the key ways in which social media influences conflict narratives is through the spread of propaganda and misinformation.

In the chaotic and fast-paced environment of a civil war, it can be difficult to discern truth from fiction, especially when false information is spread at lightning speed across various social media channels.

This can lead to the distortion of reality and the manipulation of public opinion, further exacerbating tensions and fueling the flames of conflict.

Another aspect of social media's influence on conflict narratives is its ability to amplify the voices of marginalized groups and provide a platform for the documentation of human rights abuses. In many modern civil wars, civilians are often the most affected by violence and oppression, and social media allows them to share their stories with the world, garnering international attention and support. This can be a double-edged sword, however, as the dissemination of graphic images and videos can also desensitize viewers and further perpetuate the cycle of violence.

Moreover, social media has played a significant role in mobilizing civilian populations and organizing protests and resistance movements during civil wars.

Platforms like Facebook and Twitter (X) have been instrumental in coordinating humanitarian aid efforts, disseminating information about safe zones, and connecting displaced individuals with resources and support networks.

However, this level of connectivity also comes with risks, as governments and armed groups can use social media to track and target dissenters, leading to further violence and repression.

In conclusion, the impact of social media on conflict narratives in modern civil wars cannot be overstated. While these platforms have the potential to amplify marginalized voices, document human rights abuses, and mobilize civilian populations, they also have the power to spread propaganda, and misinformation, and incite further violence.

As we navigate the complexities of contemporary warfare, it is crucial for adults to critically evaluate the information they consume on social media and to be aware of the ways in which these platforms can shape our understanding of conflict.

Leveraging Social Platforms for Advocacy or Disinformation

In today's modern world, social platforms have become powerful tools for advocacy and spreading information, but they can also be used for disinformation and manipulation. As we navigate through the complexities of modern civil wars, it is crucial to understand how these platforms can be leveraged for both positive and negative purposes.

Advocacy on social platforms can be a powerful force for change in civil conflicts. Activists and organizations can use these platforms to raise awareness about injustices, mobilize support for their cause, and organize protests and demonstrations.

By harnessing the power of social media, individuals can amplify their voices and reach a global audience, sparking international outrage and pressure on governments to address human rights abuses.

However, the flip side of this coin is the spread of disinformation and propaganda on social platforms. In modern civil wars, misinformation and fake news can be used to manipulate public opinion, incite violence, and sow discord among opposing factions.

It is essential for individuals to critically evaluate the information they consume on social media and verify its accuracy before sharing it with others.

As we prepare for the challenges of modern civil wars, it is important to be aware of the role that social platforms play in shaping public discourse and influencing political outcomes. By understanding how these platforms can be used for advocacy or disinformation, we can better navigate the complex landscape of contemporary conflicts and work toward positive change.

In conclusion, social platforms have the potential to be powerful tools for advocacy in modern civil wars, but they also pose risks in terms of spreading disinformation and propaganda. As we engage with these platforms, it is essential to be vigilant and discerning in our consumption of information, and to use our voices responsibly to promote peace, justice, and human rights in the face of conflict.

Safeguarding Your Online Presence During Civil Unrest

In today's modern world, civil unrest and conflict have become increasingly common occurrences. With the rise of social media and technology, it is more important than ever to safeguard your online presence during times of civil unrest. This subchapter will explore the various ways in which you can protect yourself online and ensure that your personal information remains secure.

One of the first steps in safeguarding your online presence during civil unrest is to be mindful of the information you share on social media platforms. During times of conflict, it is easy for misinformation to spread quickly, and sharing personal details or location information can put you at risk. Be cautious about what you post online and consider adjusting your privacy settings to limit who can see your posts.

Additionally, it is important to be aware of the potential for cyber warfare during times of civil unrest. Hackers and other malicious actors may attempt to infiltrate your devices or accounts to gather information or disrupt communication networks. Be sure to use strong, unique passwords for all your online accounts and consider using two-factor authentication for an added layer of security.

Furthermore, consider the use of virtual private networks (VPNs) to protect your online activity and mask your IP address. VPNs encrypt your internet connection, making it more difficult for hackers or government agencies to track your online movements. This can be especially important during times of civil unrest when internet censorship or monitoring may be prevalent.

Lastly, stay informed about the latest developments in technology and security measures to ensure that you are prepared for any potential threats to your online presence. By taking proactive steps to protect yourself online, you can navigate through civil unrest with confidence and peace of mind. Remember, your safety and security should always be a top priority, both online and offline.

Chapter 12

Conclusion: Building Your Modern Civil War Survival Plan

In conclusion, building a modern civil war survival plan is crucial in today's uncertain world. With the constant threat of conflict looming, it is important for adults to be prepared and aware of the potential dangers they may face.

By understanding the modern civil war landscape and the various factors at play, individuals can better equip themselves to navigate through such turbulent times.

One of the key aspects to consider when building a survival plan is being aware of modern civil war trends and what to watch out for.

From urban warfare tactics to technological advancements in warfare, knowing the potential threats can help individuals stay one step ahead and be prepared for any situation that may arise.

Furthermore, the rise of cyber warfare and its implications in modern conflicts cannot be ignored. Understanding the role of technology in warfare and how it can impact civilians is essential for developing a comprehensive survival plan.

Additionally, the use of drones and unmanned aerial vehicles in warfare adds another layer of complexity to the modern battlefield, requiring individuals to be knowledgeable about these advancements and how to protect themselves from potential attacks.

Moreover, the role of private military companies in contemporary conflicts and the impact of social media on modern civil wars cannot be overlooked. These factors play a significant role in shaping the modern battlefield and must be taken into consideration when developing a survival plan. By understanding the various aspects of modern civil war conflicts, individuals can better prepare themselves for the challenges that may lie ahead.

In conclusion, building a modern civil war survival plan requires a comprehensive understanding of the various factors at play in today's conflicts. By being informed about the modern civil war landscape and the potential threats that may arise, individuals can better prepare themselves for any situation that may come their way. With the right knowledge and preparation, adults can navigate through modern civil wars with resilience and strength.

Top 10 things to know when preparing for survival

(This outline is loosely based on a book by Blake Hargreaves – Prepping 101)

1. Identify the threat near you.
2. Define your survival objectives.
3. Assess your needs for long-term survival.
4. Stockpile essential supplies (see list below).
5. Acquire and develop skills needed to live and thrive:

a. Basic survivalist training.

b. Weapons training.

c. Medical training.

d. Growing your food.

6. Determine your long-term shelter options.

7. Secure your environment.

8. Create an evacuation plan (move to an alternate location).

9. Establish communication and networking.

10. Prepare, practice, review, and refine:

    a. Maintain secrecy about your prepping and supply line.

    b. Prioritize your family's safety and well-being.

Top Things You Need on Your Survival Prep Checklist

1. Survivalist paperback guidebooks with checklists. *(Prepping 101 - Blake Hargreaves)*

2. Hand weapons and plenty of ammo.
3. Freshwater or bottled water source.
4. Food - Ready-meal style packets.
5. Paper items: toilet paper, paper plates, utensils, etc.
6. Lighter and fluid, portable stove/heater.
7. Medical kit and instructions for any type of injury.
8. Maintenance medicines.
9. Flashlights with plenty of spare batteries.
10. Handheld walkie-talkies with plenty of batteries.
11. Hand tools (not power tools).
12. Basic home repair guidebooks (paper books).
13. Extra clothing and bedding for all seasons.
14. Paperback books for long-term situations.

About the author

Author Bio: Del McCool aka D.G. McCool Jr.

Del McCool is an indie author who publishes his works under the San-del Writers brand. His passion for writing began in his early school days when he cultivated a love for storytelling. Del's literary repertoire primarily includes fiction, science fiction, and paranormal mystery stories.

Del served in the US Army for ten years, spending six of those years in West Germany along the Iron Curtain. Following his military service, he transitioned to a career in law enforcement, where he dedicated 14 years. He then spent the next 24 years working in the corporate world, while continuing to pursue his writing part-time.

Del is married to Sandra, and they have seven children.

Indie Author

In 2010, Del co-authored the book "Future Conquests" and played a key role in getting it published later.

Since 2021, he has been actively writing and publishing books across several online platforms. Del McCool's diverse life experiences enrich his storytelling, bringing a unique depth and authenticity to his work.

Scan Here

Printed in Great Britain
by Amazon

48648995R00066